MW00883652

The Positive Leader: Reflections & Motivations

Dr. Kenneth Morton

The Positive Leader: Reflections & Motivations
All Rights Reserved.
Copyright © 2021 Dr. Kenneth Morton
v4.0

The opinions expressed in this manuscript are solely the opinions of the author and do not represent the opinions or thoughts of the publisher. The author has represented and warranted full ownership and/or legal right to publish all the materials in this book.

This book may not be reproduced, transmitted, or stored in whole or in part by any means, including graphic, electronic, or mechanical without the express written consent of the publisher except in the case of brief quotations embodied in critical articles and reviews.

Outskirts Press, Inc.
http://www.outskirtspress.com

Paperback ISBN: 978-1-9772-0561-2

Cover Photo © 2021 www.gettyimages.com. All rights reserved - used with permission.

Outskirts Press and the "OP" logo are trademarks belonging to Outskirts Press, Inc.

PRINTED IN THE UNITED STATES OF AMERICA

Table of Contents

Also available from the author

Defined by Attitude: The Power of Positivity
Outskirts Press

Your 365-Day Journal of Positive Affirmations and Commitments
Outskirts Press

Foreword

Get Excited!!!... because the book you are now holding in your hands will empower your life. The wisdom shared throughout this book will transform you.

I know that's a bold statement. However, it's the absolute TRUTH.

When I first read Kenneth Morton's **"Positive Leader: Reflections and Motivations"**, I was amazed that each of his 33 messages spoke directly to my heart and mind.

Trust me, this book will bless you.

Kenneth's writing style is so captivating that he has the gift in awakening your consciousness to the essence of true leadership.

As a professional keynote speaker who has given presentations in 45 states and 18 countries, I have interacted with the "best of the best" thought leaders and authors. And this is why I have so much excitement regarding this amazing book because it has made a difference by inspiring me to "step up" my leadership commitment.

Get Ready!... Get Ready!... Get Ready!... to be inspired to take your life to a higher level because this book will remind you of the greatness within you.

Each of these 33 passages approach leadership from a different perspective. The real-life, nuggets of wisdom will cause you to reflect and go deeper in your intentions as a positive leader.

As you read each one, I encourage you to apply the wisdom in your daily life. By applying what you've learned, you will reinforce winning leadership principles and manifest even greater results.

This is an Exciting Opportunity for you to implement what you've read and see the power of this book real-time in real ways. And to really make this book come alive, feel free to share your top-3 with your family and friends so they also grow as a positive leader.

Thank you Kenneth for writing this empowering book. It is having a ripple effect.
Live With Purpose!

Marlon Smith
www.SuccessByChoice.com

Acknowledgements and Dedication

This part of my book is where I seize the opportunity to express my sincerest thanks and appreciation to all those who provided me with encouragement, constructive critique, feedback, love appreciation and life experiences that continues to influence my worldview. I feel blessed with the opportunity to continue walking in my purpose that my heavenly father created uniquely for me. Writing is a journey, and I cannot make the trip without those closest to me. To know me is to know that I am all about family. I am honored to show my thanks and appreciation to my wife Tracy and our daughter Kamdyn. Individually and together, you provide me with much to reflect upon and consistently motivate me to be my best self. I love you both.

Continuing in the family theme I thank my father, the late Mr. Robert L. Morton, Sr. and my mother, the late Mrs. Dorothy J. Morton for your love, support, and guidance throughout my life. My mother transitioned from this life during the completion of this book. She would periodically ask me how my writing was coming along and looked forward to seeing it and reading it. Mom, I hoped that this edition would have made you proud. To both mom and dad, I would not be where I am without the positive influence that you continue to have on me. I love you. I also want to send a public show of appreciation to my *mother and father-in-love*, the late Mr. Norfleet Vinson and Mrs. Susie Vinson. Your love and support mean the world to me and I will always appreciate both of you. Many thanks to my dear siblings, cousins, nephews, nieces, and to the many members of my family who are no longer with us in an earthly realm.

For me, family extends beyond blood in many instances. Deep appreciation goes out to my "Mountain Top" Family, my YBLA Family, and to my true friends and colleagues who continue to support me and my desire to walk in my purpose. I must show heartfelt appreciation to my ITSMF Family and of course to my fellow members of The Mighty 33, my ITSMF Management Associate Cohort. Many thanks to my coaches, mentors, and trusted advisors who continue pouring into me. I have nothing but gratitude for all that you do in challenging me to be my absolute best and to go for it! Gratitude within my spirit is what I feel towards each of you.

As I reflect upon everyone who made this work possible, I dedicate this work to you.

Introduction

It is my pleasure to introduce you to my work, *Positive Leader: Reflections and Motivations*! Throughout my life-journey, I am continually intrigued by all that I am fortunate to encounter. People and situations have a way of literally and figuratively speaking to your heart, your mind and in some instances your soul. I am sure that your life also provides you with much to reflect upon and a great deal of motivations for your present and future path. I decided to assemble thirty-three of my experiences to share with you. I am both grateful and excited that you are taking the time to indulge me.

Many such encounters provide wonderful mental threads for us to marvel at; thoughts and realizations that had an uplifting influence upon us. Those items are pleasant reflections of the past. We enjoy the opportunity to retrace those steps and revisit those times. Life can be great and there is greatness within you. When those two conditions meet, the outcome can be powerful. We also know that life is not perfect and situations do not always work out in a good manner. People may disappoint us, things may not work out as planned and events sometimes go off the rails.

Reflections and Motivations is a chance to consider positive approaches to a few topics that can have a major impact upon your life. I often think of writing as an opportunity to engage in an important dialogue with my readers. I share my perspectives to provide you with thoughts and insights to help you through challenges as a leader. It is my desire for you to reflect upon the items found within that resonate with your journey and I also challenge you to walk away with a fresh perspective that motivates you to move forward in a positive way. If either or both of those conditions are satisfied, the dialogue created through this work serves the proper purpose.

Positive leader, get ready to reflect and get ready to become motivated. Loose yourself in a few revelations and stories, then pre-pare to enhance your life journey with these insights. I trust that you will enjoy my writing and as always, I look forward to hearing your thoughts and perspectives.

> *Positivity and negativity seldom ride in the same car. When they do, negativity is always in the back seat. The only way that you will see negativity is either when you turn around or when you momentarily glance into your rear-view mirror. In both instances, negativity is right where it belongs, behind you!*

I will now get out of your way to allow your reflections and mo-tivation to begin!

Make an external impact using your internal positivity. Make it known!

Image by Clark Tibbs

1

Hey leader…your words matter!

Whether written on paper, spoken from one person to another, delivered in an auditorium with thousands in attendance or conveyed via Skype, Twitter or any other social media post; your words matter. As you are reading this right now, you are a testimony to the fact that words matter. The same is true with each and every word that I write, thus I want to make valuable use of your time and attention. After all this collection is an assembly of words brought together to highlight or provide relevant perspectives on topics introduced to my audience.

Leaders, we know that one of our most important roles is to be an effective communicator. Most of us have seen the beauty and harmony created when the right words are combined and delivered with the proper tone and at the right time. Conversely, we have also seen the train wreck created when one is not careful with word choice, tone, or the timing of when their message is conveyed.

We have communicated with others since a very young age and it is easy to take how we choose and use our words for granted. **The meanings and ideas we communicate through our words are the currency that we use in the marketplace called life, and enables each of us to articulate our thoughts, feelings and values.** Even when we repeat something said by another individual, we are often associated with similar thoughts or we may become inseparably associated with the same thoughts as they come out of our mouth.

If we believe that our words are currency in life, we owe it to ourselves to choose and use our words wisely. Our words have the power to build up the downtrodden. Our words have the ability to send your team or your organization forward, energized in ways that will amaze everyone. Our words can speak truth to power which can yield outstanding results. While we should be realist and not "candy coat" what is truthfully happening, we as leaders should always strive to be 100% authentic while choosing and using our words properly.

Take some time and reflect upon how your words have guided your interactions with others. Were you effective and authentic? Did you convey your message with clarity? Did you build up or tear down those whom you interacted with? Were you able to help another individual get out of the ditch and back on the right road as a result of how you used your words?

Once you reflect upon previous interactions, I ask that you proactively think about how you will enhance your leadership profile through better word management. Make the commitment to master what comes from you and how it is conveyed. Those whom you interact with and lead will appreciate it and see you as a more effective leader!

2

Follow the Doctor's Prescription

Periodically, people ask me if all of my positive thoughts and writings are real. I've been asked, "Doc..how are you able to stay in the positivity zone? Does anything ever pull you down or cause you to fall from your positive place?" My simple response usually goes as follows: a) yes, I am human and I experience ups and downs the same as everyone else, b) people and events provide me with negative vibes and sometimes negative feelings, and c) just because negativity is in the atmosphere neither means that I have to embrace it nor gravitate towards it.

For me; it is all about choice. I am the gatekeeper of what I allow to get inside of me. My responsibility is to prevent negativity from taking up permanent residence within my spirit. **I choose to remain positive.** The key to making this happen is to follow Dr. Morton's prescription and I will share it with you now. *On a daily basis, infuse positivity into the little things in order to make a big difference in your life.* One cannot merely think positive thoughts and expect it materialize. We must bring positivity to life daily. When we integrate positivity into our daily routines, we make a difference as a leader.

Perhaps you are thinking that with all that is on your plate there is no room or time available to make this happen. I am willing to bet that you **can** fit positivity into your life as it is today. I am always amazed by the reaction received when I call a cashier by his or her name as displayed on the nametag. In looking to go beyond just a name, I like to use their name to issue a lighthearted compliment or to say something uplifting and encouraging. On occasion when leaving the office, I run into the cleaning crew. Many times, they seem to appreciate when I take the time to speak, smile and ask how their evening is going. Neither act requires great thought nor a herculean level of effort to bring positivity to others. Here is the healing and restorative power in my prescription; *when you infuse positivity into your daily routines and consistently uplift others it becomes hard to keep it from yourself.*

I take my own advice and follow my own prescription. I encourage you, positive leader to do the same. Whenever you see pharmaceutical advertisements they always provide you with a long list of possible side-effects. It is my duty to warn you of the possible side-effects of following my prescription:

1. An increased sense of personal happiness and self-fulfillment.

2. Greater personal positivity.

3. Increased levels of positivity in the lives of those whom you interact with.

4. More satisfying engagements with those whom you choose to interact with.

5. Positive expectations for a brighter future.

When you follow the Dr.'s prescription, you may get a smile in return and some people will immediately let you know how much you uplifted them. Even if the response is not a good one, you can feel good knowing that you made the effort.

In our social media laced world, it is very easy to agree with someone else's positive statement or their words on our device. We can effortlessly "like" an image or their perspective. I invite you to get out of your comfort zone, take your medicine then act! Follow the Dr.'s orders and rest assured that there is neither a deductible to meet nor a lifetime positivity limit that you should worry about reaching. Your benefits are priceless and endless.

3

Don't Doubt: Do!

Positive leader, this is your time! Now is the moment for your work and your efforts to come together in a way that produces the outcome you are pursuing. One of the most powerful threats that can stand between where you began and where want to go is the enemy of doubt.

Doubt can render you motionless in your quest to achieve your dreams. Doubt can also slow your momentum to a snail's pace and call into question all of your well-intentioned plans. We must remain steadfast in our efforts and keep moving to complete our goals and ensure that we take care of our priorities. We must not doubt, **we must do!** We cannot afford to become prey to the predator called doubt. It is imperative that our forward progress does not fall apart and that we continue moving down the path to success.

Doing is what results in growth and improvement. Even slow, consistent advancement towards your goals is worthy progress. It is human to have moments of question, that is normal. Winners never remain in depths of doubt. Take your place among those who are doing and taking the proper actions to make it happen. You will be pleased with your efforts and progress.

4

Develop Your Positivity Network

Often when one thinks of networking, thoughts immediately begin to consider an event or meeting with others. As a verb, networking involves making connections with others both personally and professionally. As a noun, your network is an important element in your success structure and your innermost framework. Your network should be filled with a diverse group of people with varied skills and interests. This is important so that as you learn and grow from your network, your interactions are not fed from a group of monolithic individuals. Great value is derived when we interact and share ideas with others who are not carbon copies of ourselves.

When assembling your network, always consider your positive mindset and your desire to surround yourself with other positive people. I am not suggesting that your network should only have "yes-men" or "yes-women" who always agree with your every thought or words expressed. There is value achieved when challenged to expand our thinking and it can be done in a positive and constructive way. Surround yourself with people who are moving through life with a contagious, positive outlook. Think about the level of optimism you regularly choose to associate yourself with. Do you wish to interact with individuals who are moving forward and will also challenge and inspire you to be your very best? The fact that I have your attention leads me to believe that you are that type of person.

Choose carefully who you allow within your inner network, your positivity circle. Make sure that you are delivering positivity to the equation. I believe that once you commit to a life of positivity, you will insist upon surrounding yourself with other like-minded people. Why would you want to do anything else?

Allow your positivity to spread beyond the limits of
what you can see. Create a lasting legacy.

Image by Janusz Maniak

5

Positivity Requires Persistence

Have you ever labored on a task that required you to give it your all each and every day? Most of us can think of a few items on our never-ending to-do list that may challenge us in this manner. One of the items that may be on your list requiring constant work and attention is challenging yourself to achieve and maintain a consistently high level of positivity through all that you encounter daily. Let's face it, life brings a lot to deal with and is often extremely tough to navigate. We encounter complex situations and people, along with many competing priorities. Often, we are forced to address drama that we neither created nor align with. It all may make you want to throw up your hands and shout enough!

We know that we were not created to feel like victims while moving through life's challenges. We can feel very confident that the often negative or challenging circumstances that surround us does not in any way define us. After all, **where I am** (in the middle of a mess) **is not who I am!** In order to keep negativity at bay and operate as positive individuals, we must develop a stubborn level of persistence. We are accountable to ourselves to make sure that we operate from a place of positivity and that we are ready to turn back negative notions and influences that approach us. Sometimes, we are introduced to a thought that we should not allow to take residence within our being. Other times, negativity may come from another individual or groups of individuals whom we should not allow to unduly influence us.

Our constant and persistent pursuit to remain positive in no way guarantees that negativity will not come our way. Our persistence to remain positive should become a lifestyle that allows us to work through our challenges. Ideally, our level of persistence develops into a routine that helps us in future situations.

I ask that you think about what is required to employ the level of persistence needed to achieve and maintain a high level of positivity in your life. You will likely get greater joy from the things that you do, and others are likely to appreciate you more when you operate from your positive platform. Get ready to invest in your fair share of sweat equity to make it happen. Adapting positivity is not always an easy choice. The journey begins with your belief that you can make it happen, then get it done! I believe that you are ready for the task, beginning today.

6

Always in Season

We do not always have to look at the calendar to know when seasons change. Every season serves an important purpose in the cycle of life. The thought of spring conjures images of lush green plants, budding trees, flowers in bloom, birds nesting, and grass thickening. Additionally, in spring the days are longer compared to winter and the extended sunlight is really nice in the evenings. We know what we expect to see and how we expect to feel about spring, even before it arrives.

We can draw comparisons between weather conditions and our lives. Sometimes, the weather may appear to be out of season. Thoughts of snowball fights and visions of kids building snow forts are appropriate during winter in some locations. The same activities are out of place in other places or at different times. Situations and challenges that we face daily may have us feeling a bit out of season. It is not hard for a few tough encounters or challenging conversations to have us feeling as though we are in the wrong place at the wrong time. When will the weather break in our lives and bring the warm days that we long to see once again?

As rough as many situations may seem, they are not always as awful as they appear. Just as a spring snow may seem out of place, so are our challenges. We know what we want to see and often, we know exactly where we desire to be at a point in time. Plants have a messaging system which keeps them alive and allows them to conserve their energy when an out-of-season snow lies on the ground. We also have an internal messaging system which keep us vibrant and ready to go in the midst of our challenges. Our level of **positivity** can keep us always *in season* even when the *blizzards* in our life bring strong winds and problematic drifts. Beneath the layers of challenge, positivity keeps each of us standing strong.

Our approach to life is largely determined by our mindset, our attitude towards people and situations happening around us all the time. We must remember that regardless of how situations may appear, we are never out of season. When situations cause us to appear out of season, we are always relevant and always in season. Freshly fallen snow will not last forever. Regardless of whether challenges resemble flurries or deep drifts, they will soon disappear. We know the stories of individuals who trek through deep snow and treacherous conditions to reach their destinations. Through our out-of-season situations, we must employ that same resolve.

We must remain encouraged and refuse to believe that our winterlike conditions will last forever. This is your season and this is my season. Warmer days are on the way. During these times, our positivity keeps us thriving and learning. We are positive leaders at all times, not just during favorable conditions. Remain focused and continue making a positive impact on the world. Know that you are always in season, regardless of how it looks.

7

Define Your Success

We are well aware that life is about choices and our path to our success or failure is defined by the choices we make. I believe so strongly in the power of choice that I dedicated a whole chapter dealing with choices in my book, *Defined by Attitude: The Power of Positivity*. We know that choice sets us on a path and creates conditions for outcomes to occur, ideally desirable outcomes. We strategize, plan and work hard to make progress towards our goals and reach our success measures as positive leaders. Actions taken and behaviors lived, which support our success, must be deeply intertwined with who we are and the values we possess.

An important decision that we must carefully make is the way that we choose to define our success. When we set out on a path to achieve greatness, we need to ensure that we are measuring ourselves in a manner that is accurate and meaningful. I must constantly take inventory of who I am, what skills and competencies I possess and what I desire to accomplish. The impact that I wish to make and how I judge myself as successful are important considerations. This becomes important since I do not want to spend a lifetime falling short of success measures that are either unattainable or worse, striving towards success levels that someone else erroneously defined for me. **The standard we choose to measure ourselves means everything**.

By now, you are aware that I believe that when you approach a task, initiative or another person with positivity; great things can happen. That is where I live. I am also a realist and believe that each of us must understand how we define our success. When we align our purpose and actions with attaining goals that we believe in, our inner passion is ignited. Life is big and every person has the responsibility to understand what defines and drives the pursuit of their success.

There are countless stories of individuals who have the look of success yet live miserable lives. The look of success may be in the form of expensive trinkets, powerful career titles, the ability to influence others or in the car that one drives. Other success measures may include how much volunteer time one may give or their ability to adequately provide for his or her family. My point is that success is uniquely understood and defined for each of us.

There once was a highly accomplished doctor who did extremely well in the medical field. She effortlessly sailed through undergraduate school and medical school, finishing at the top of each class. No one was surprised by her success and many individuals would have willingly switched places with her in a heartbeat. She lived in a great house and was highly respected in the medical community. It sounds as though her life was filled with success. By many measures, her life was filled with many milestone accomplishments. The problem with this story is that she saw her life as a miserable existence. Success as measured by many others was unbearable. Our doctor was tops in her field, however she chose her profession as a way to fulfill the wishes of her parents who were both doctors. Additional pressure from home was provided by two older siblings, also doctors.

In this short story, we see that our main character chose success measures defined by others and ignored her passions and where her heart told her she should go. Finally, misery became so intense that our doctor made a career change and became an artist. Armed with newfound goals and success measures, our doctor soon became successful and happy doing what she wanted to do. She freed herself from the constraints of fulfilling levels of success that others defined for her. Through her realignment, true success was defined and achieved.

I challenge you to reexamine your understanding of what you deem as successful and how you choose to define yourself as successful. It is important that we vigorously chase worthwhile passions and goals, aligned with who we are. I believe that there is greatness in each of us. I believe in the power of positivity. I also believe that happiness is reached when our definition of success is in synch with who we authentically are or strive to become. Life is full of choices and how we define our success is an important one. Be very thoughtful as you contemplate what you wish to achieve and what success looks like when you get there. Run your race and do not get caught-up chasing another's success. Last and certainly not least, infuse massive amounts of positivity in your pursuit of success. It makes all the difference. In a positive way, choose carefully.

8

Raising the Bar

Our journey through life presents us with many moments of anticipation, challenge, joy, surprise, exasperation, disappointment and sometimes fear. While enduring all that comes our way, it is healthy to periodically pause to consider our status and our path to continued forward progress. While some are *"ok"* with where they are in life, others invest time thinking about how to raise the bar in identified areas to achieve next-level performance and success. This sort of planning and introspective thinking is healthy and essential to achieve consistent and sustained growth. As we know, good health and positive growth keeps us living and thriving.

When raising your bar, be sure to challenge yourself in a reasonable way. You may wish to leverage setting S.M.A.R.T. goals in order to raise your bar. The S.M.A.R.T. methodology employs the following guidelines we should incorporate when goal-setting.

Specific- Clearly define what you set out to achieve

Measurable- Predetermine how you will measure progress and goal achievement

Attainable- Keep goals motivating, yet within the realm of what is possible

Realistic- Ensure that goals are reasonable for what you are able to accomplish

Time-bound- Determine and set the timeline to achieve your stated goals

Investing the time to create and document goals using a S.M.A.R.T. approach can make all the difference in wishing for goal achievement and actually reaching goal achievement.

Your approach to raising your bar should include a right attitude and a high level of positivity. Both are important and required. Few achievements worth gaining were ever accomplished with an "I can't mentality." When someone overcomes insurmountable odds and prevails, the turnaround begins with an attitude to succeed. Raise your bar with confidence and commit yourself to work diligently to reach your goals. Yes; there is work involved and the effort required for breakthrough may be enormous. Merely raising the bar without putting in the effort is not a winning recipe.

Believe in your **"I can"**, commit to your **"I will"**, then take positive action to create the story which will one day tell the world what **"you did."** Before you know it, you will return to your next moment of pause to raise your bar, with positivity of course!

*Through periods of uncertainty, remain true to your values
and beliefs. They are your barriers of protection.*

Image by Martin Fennema

9

How Might I Assist?

This short story is about an individual who made a journey several times a week to walk to the store for food or sometimes to the pharmacy to pick up necessary medicines. For others, the walk would not have been excessively long. The individual on foot did not walk very fast and the routine trips were especially taxing during extreme weather conditions. One day, a woman who lived nearby stopped in her vehicle while passing our traveler on foot. The woman driving her car previously passed our traveler several times, yet she never considered offering assistance. This particular day, she pulled over and introduced herself. She mentioned observing many times what seemed to be a taxing trip and the struggle to walk home with numerous packages.

The person walking was so surprised that someone noticed them and that someone thought enough to see if any assistance was needed. This individual lived alone and did not have very many friends; thus, they were very appreciative. Additionally, there was no one to call to help with the required trips. After a short while, these two individuals formed a strong friendship and regular trips by car were planned.

You may ask by now, what does such a story have to do with being a positive leader? Our driver saw a challenging situation and knew that she had an opportunity to significantly improve the life of another person. She willingly helped without being asked. She literally and figuratively carried another individual to a better place as a result of her intervention. She took on the role of a positive leader to improve another's life and immediate situation.

In our busy lives, how many situations do we overlook daily where our willingness to assist could make a great difference? How many people do we see and interact with who would immensely appreciate if we would only take time and offer our help? How many individuals and situations do we routinely see, yet choose to ignore especially when it is not convenient for us to help? Positive leaders look for opportunities to assist others and make a difference. No human has the answer to every challenge and certainly not everyone in need will accept help. For certain, **we are all better off when we work together** to overcome life's challenges and being a positive leader when assisting someone else is a great way to engage. Sometimes, an offer to assist is refused. We may never know how our offer will be received until we try.

Beginning today, let us develop the habit of looking for opportunities to get out of our comfort zones and help someone else. Just like our driver, positive leaders get involved and make a tangible difference without an expectation of reward or recognition. Make your brand of positive leadership real in the life of someone else. It is now our turn to drive someone else forward in their journey. **Together, we win!**

10

Positive Leader...
Celebrate Yourself!

I learn many lessons from the advice of mentors and trusted advisors in my journey. As an avid reader, I also observe what contributes to the success of other people. I am fully comfortable in my own skin and I am not in any way looking to be a carbon-copy of anyone else. There is however wisdom gained when we observe tried and true strategies and best-practices which may fit into our own program.

One such practice that I observed from a mentor is to make sure that I spend quality time celebrating myself and I encourage you to do the same by celebrating yourself. As you already know, being a positive leader is no easy task. There are constant demands of our time and attention. Some may seek us out for the value and insight that we bring into the room when considering important proposals or when problem solving. Leaders should be effective communicators, so it may be our ability to articulate complex topics or the manner that we listen with empathy and respond in an appropriate manner nearly every time. I stress the word nearly. Even as positive leaders, no one is perfect.

Not everything that occupies our capacity is negative. Many hours are filled coaching and advising others to assist in their development and well-being. We may be consulted to make a difference on a large project or to bring home final plans for a festive and fun event. We also invest a great deal of well-spent time and attention celebrating others; which is always a great thing to do.

There was an individual who was highly regarded within their inner circle among close friends. Even from afar, others who had limited interaction with this leader also thought very well of the same individual and also held them in high regard. This individual generously gave time, talent, treasure and sacrificed to ensure that others received their best attention, an immediate response and ongoing follow-up to resolve whatever challenge presented. When it came time to celebrate other people's achievements and goals, our leader was consistently right there. Many who knew this person generally appreciated the relationship and support. While some may believe that too much of a good thing is never an issue, we can be dreadfully out of balance. You see, our leader spent so much time pouring into others, they failed to pour inwardly by celebrating their own progress and successes along the way.

We must take time to give proper attention to ourselves, which includes celebrating what we do and how we accomplish our goals to make necessary progress through life. This feeds our ability to maintain our high levels of positivity and well-being. Consider the value of celebrating progress and achievements. If we as leaders invest all that we have into everything and everyone else without replenishing ourselves, eventually we become bankrupt. We should develop a healthy network of others who also make timely deposits into our celebratory account along with us. As great as having others encourage and celebrate us, we also need to ensure that a high degree of self-love and self-celebration takes place.

As you navigate through the next few days and weeks, take some time and celebrate yourself. It does not always have to be at the very end of a project or personal initiative, sometimes, a well-placed measure of self-celebration is the very thing needed to help you reach completion. I encourage you to look for and plan how you will recognize key moments in your life. Plan in advance your reward when a goal is attained or when you accomplish milestone progress in an area. **One of the best decisions you will make is to invest in yourself**. Enjoy your positive moments, after all, you are worth it.

11

Believe

Our beliefs have a tremendous impact upon whether we begin an initiative, how we move forward, and our expectations of what the end may look like. Beliefs are often shaped by our worldview, our history and what we choose to remember from past experiences. When we consider our expectations, our attitude becomes our lens for life and shapes what we think will happen.

Strong beliefs, paired with a passion for excellence is a valuable combination. We tend to gravitate toward the values that shape what we believe. It begins in each of us and provides a springboard to higher heights and next level performance. Believing in yourself is imperative when it comes to delivering anything with impact. Olympian Gail Devers captured this notion in the following words;

"Keep your dreams alive. Understand to achieve anything requires faith and belief in yourself, vision, hard work, determination, and dedication. Remember all things are possible for those who believe."

Absent thereof, others will find it hard to believe in you. Get the maximum value from your efforts and actions through your beliefs, which should be a part of our guiding principles on our journey to success.

12

A Leader's Confidence

There are myriad approaches to leadership and how one should behave or act while serving in a leadership role. Adding another level of complexity to this topic is the fact that there are formal and informal leaders within the various organizations and businesses where we choose to work or volunteer our time. Sometimes, formal leaders are created due to the logistics of the organizational chart. Informal leaders are typically created due to the level of respect that others have for an individual based upon subject-matter knowledge or personal effectiveness. It has been stated that an important measure of a leader is the level of followership that he or she develops in those who choose to follow.

Successfully functioning as a leader requires one to approach their role and responsibilities with confidence. This may sound as though I am stating the obvious, however it is always amazing how many leaders exude a lack of confidence in their approach. Confidence does not imply that one has all of the answers or that one does not ever require help. In fact, a confident leader knows when to seek assistance or input from others as well as when to be transparent enough to recognize that personal knowledge and ability may not be sufficient to make decisions with a high level of confidence. Believe it or not, reaching out for assistance when needed may enhance how you are viewed as a leader.

Levels of confidence in leaders may be exhibited and perceived in various ways. It could be in how critical messages are conveyed and the tone in which they are delivered. Confidence may be conveyed in the time it takes a leader to make important decisions. Many of us could make a more confident decision in most situations if we were given additional information or another week to arrive at a conclusion. We may not always have the luxury of additional intelligence or incremental time to figure it out. Leaders are often tasked with making key decisions and moving forward with less than complete information in an abbreviated timeline. Leaders are compelled to move forward with confidence under those conditions.

Leadership in action likely means something different to various people if you were to ask them to describe their experience with a confident leader. One may recall her military experience when the senior officer looked into the eyes of the troops and issued the command to charge forward with less than perfect knowledge of conditions ahead. Another may describe a work-related project when many depended upon keen analysis from a single individual to inform the broader team about an issue prior to moving forward or taking action. In other instances, perhaps a team of individuals have the task to discuss and decide critical next-steps in large multidimensional project. Whatever the scenario, those functioning as leaders are in their role to make decisions with confidence. After all, every leader's goal should be to earn trust from those being led and every follower truly wants to have trust in those who are leading them. Confidence goes a long way in helping a leader earn trust and may secure it in the eyes of those being led.

Here are a few examples of what confidence looks like? Confidence is the manner that each leader makes decisions and operates on a daily basis. Confidence is also the ability to engage in healthy debate with others throughout the organization without feeling threatened by thoughts or ideas that may differ from your own. A leader's confidence also comes through in his or her ability to speak about what they are planning to do, then follow through to complete the task or action. True confidence is neither imitated nor faked. Confidence is real and is validated by what one does and how one does it. While an individual may fool some for a short period of time (if at all); a leader's confidence is authentic and stands the test of time. Notice, I did not refer to the first individual as a leader. I saved that designation for the second individual who consistently displays authentic confidence.

Lastly, confidence is not justification to be pompous or arrogant. Both of those characteristics pave the way for one's downfall. Let's make it our goal each and every day to move and act with confidence in all that we do. Isn't that the type of individual we would want to follow? That is also an important trait that those following us seek.

Your positive light can always shine through, regardless of what negative forces attempt to accomplish.

Image by Sharon Pittaway

13

S.M.A.R.T. Goal Setting with Positivity

Previously, I encouraged all Positive Leaders to employ a S.M.A.R.T. approach when establishing **S**pecific, **M**easurable, **A**ttainable, **R**ealistic, **T**imebound goals. I will go a bit further to discuss integrating positivity into your S.M.A.R.T. approach.

With a positive approach, set your mind upon your **s**pecific goals. Know what you are pursuing and organize your plan that will create your desired result. This level of focus will enable you to direct your energy upon the right tasks and challenges.

Understand and **m**easure your next-level goals in positive terms. Too often, people measure themselves in terms of what they did not achieve. If you consistently think about the 5% that you missed, when will you ever celebrate the 95% gained? Achieving positive success measures becomes important, especially when the journey becomes rough. Celebrate progress along the way, however never lose your drive to reach your goals with excellence.

In positive terms, are your goals **a**ttainable? Are you committed to tirelessly working to achieve what you set out to do? An achievable mindset is a positive mindset. Success begins within you. If you do not believe that your goals are achievable, who else should or will believe that you will achieve your goals?

When it comes to setting *r*ealistic goals, be careful and leverage positivity with balance to ensure that you are not in pursuit of the unrealistic. Challenge yourself and keep in mind what is realistic for you to achieve. We were not designed to run every race in life, therefore, every success is not ours to attain. While we are aware of our super power (attitude) and have all of the "can do" that one can muster, a great reality check validates and explores whether our goals are realistic.

*T*ime is our last step when constructing strong S.M.A.R.T. goals. Use positive thoughts and considerations when you evaluate the amount of time necessary to achieve your goals. When laying out your goals, are you negatively ensuring absolute failure or positively preparing a path to success based upon the time required to reach your goals? Time and proper timing are crucial elements. The right action and a great performance at the wrong time is a failed venture.

Be smart and create Positive S.M.A.R.T. goals as a path to your success! In doing so, you empower yourself to labor more efficiently and effectively towards your defined next-level. We will see you in the winner's circle.

14

I am Positively Not Waiting for Permission

My thoughts this time out of the gate are centered upon where each of us are going in life. I truly believe that you already realize the value of living with a sense of direction and purpose. Most of us are on a path whereby we aspire to do something greater or we have a desire to impact other people and situations in a fruitful manner. Few of us wake up in the morning on a path to do less or bring others down in contrast to looking for ways to lift others up. Sometimes, we may never know how much another person appreciates kind words or a smile from us during a challenging period in his or her life.

I am reminded many times of the positive impact a volunteer makes among those being assisted. I am impressed when I see someone serving at a local school to help educators with an event or by providing an additional set of watchful eyes and ears as a chaperone on a field trip. There are countless examples all around us whereby we see great people going out of their way to make life better for others. Sometimes, better comes together in a great way and other times improvement comes from taking care of small details. Every bit counts, no matter how large or how small the deed.

I look for the chance to lift others up and I do not wait for permission to do so. Each of us has an opportunity to improve the lives of others on a daily basis, and we do not need to wait for permission to do so. Everyone may not want or accept your inspiring words or well-intended deed. You may be familiar with the saying, "It is better to ask for forgiveness rather than beg for permission." I choose to take chances to inspire and encourage others. There have been a few occasions when I took the risk to help and was met with an adverse reaction. I apologized and kept moving forward undeterred. More times than not, sincere efforts to inspire are appreciated. I challenge you to do the same. If we offend another person with our brand of positivity, we can always ask for forgiveness if necessary. Let's get out of our comfort zones and avoid waiting for permission to do a good deed. Someone in your world needs to hear from you. Make it happen, extend your hand and encourage someone. They are waiting on you right now.

15

Defy Negative Gravity

Gravity is real and is not some imaginary force from a futuristic science-fiction movie or story. Without a lengthy explanation from a physicist, in an earthly frame of reference we recognize gravity as that force that pulls us back to the surface of the earth whenever we jump up or leap through the air. When rockets ignite and when planes fly through the air, enough thrust and power must be generated to over-come the force of gravity to enable flight.

Generating and applying your personal positivity can serve as your personal power to overcome the gravity of negativity. Let's face it, there are many factors and circumstances that have the ability to pull any of us down into the murky swamp of negative thoughts, feel-ings and emotions. Consider how easy it is for us to slip into negativ-ity by way of a quick and inappropriate response to another person. What about the thoughts that enter into our minds and cause im-mediate embarrassment when we realize that we said exactly how we felt loud enough to be heard by others? Or what about a time when someone whom we knew was under verbal attack and instead of standing up for them, we added to the disparaging remarks as op-posed to defending the individual?

Avoiding such negative gravity and choosing to lift-off into your realm of positivity may require a great deal of effort. While it is so easy to go to a negative place and allow negative gravity to keep you grounded, you have the ability and capacity to escape these restrictive grounding forces. I encourage you to fuel your mind with positive messages on a daily basis. Every morning, go through your pre-flight mental checklist before you start your day. Countdown and blast off into your day in a manner that enables you to escape the negative gravity that is always pulling against you. Buckle up and get ready to soar. As astronauts discovered, the view is breathtaking once you get high enough to escape our atmosphere. Imagine the view waiting for you to enjoy as you escape the atmosphere of negativity.

16

Give Yourself a Moment of Pause

Hello positive leader! I trust that you are changing the world around you with great measures of positivity and a winning attitude. It is easy for us to get caught up in the rhythm of our lives and with all of the hustle and bustle that comes along with it. After all, we are here to make a difference. I will be brief and get to my point. Give yourself a moment of pause to take in all that is going on around you. Make more meaningful interactions with others. Listen to add value as opposed to merely waiting for your opportunity to speak. And, make situations better as a result of slowing down just a bit to get in tune with your circumstances.

Yes, we are people of action and we do our best to make a positive impact. There is great value in giving yourself a moment of pause to rest, reassess and refuel. I encourage you to value the moment and take care of yourself. Pause does not mean that everything comes to a permanent halt. Just pause, marinate on the moment and refresh. I guarantee that on the other side you will be ready to move forward, renewed. Life can be a marathon, however in your race make the most of the next valuable moment that you choose!

Equipped with your positive mindset, you do not require a crowd for comfort. Positive self-confidence is refreshed in your temporary solitude. Soak it up!

Image by Benedicto de Jesus

17

Positivity Self-Help

Imagine that you have just boarded a jet destined for your favorite vacation location. You are all ready to disconnect from your daily routine for a week of rest and relaxation. Your luggage is carefully stored in the cargo area and a book that you look forward to reading is in hand. What a great start to what should be a fantastic getaway.

The jet begins pulling away from the gate and you are finally about to become airborne. A pleasant voice confidently begins to review safety and evacuation procedures with passengers in the event of an emergency. One of the first instructions communicated provides you with what should be done if the cabin loses pressure and breathing devices are deployed. Each passenger is instructed how to get their own breathing device in place prior to assisting other travelers. From a safety perspective, this is based upon the premise that one should secure his or her own safety first before helping others. Even when you attempt to act with helpful intentions, you place yourself and others at risk if you overlook this important step.

I invite you to view your attitude in the same manner. While we may have great intentions and focus upon spreading positivity to others, we must ensure that our level of positivity is where it should be before we leap into action. After all, how can we operate from a place of "verbal positivity" when our lives and our demeanor does not reflect the same? Even when we say the right words, in an attempt to inspire and uplift someone else, it rings hollow when we are not in a positive place.

Here are three steps to get you started. *First*, self-help begins with positive thoughts and a *can-do* attitude towards life. It is a posture that keeps us focused upon making interactions better through our touch points. *Second*, self-help is found in the words that we say to ourselves on a daily basis. Before we can encourage and support others, we should engage in healthy self-talk and outwardly express that we are positive people with a heart for spreading positivity to others. *Third* on this short list is your quick assessment of the real challenge that either you or your fellow traveler through life is facing. You may not have a great deal of time to complete a long assessment. In the heat of the moment, we are often compelled to quickly assess then take quick action to provide help or encouragement.

I encourage you to approach your day in the same way. Take time daily to ensure that you are ready to use your positive attitude as your lifeline. Your positivity may make the difference in a situation whereby someone's survival depends upon your capacity to assist. Ideally, in our trip through life we are surrounded by others who are ready and available to assist us when needed. Challenges and emergencies can either place us on the side of those helping or on the side of those who require help. Once all of the preflight checks and instructions are provided, you are now ready to fly. Complete your three-step checklist and get ready to travel through your day. Have a safe trip and take plenty of photos and selfies!

18

Play to Win

Positive leader, I remind you to remain laser focused upon your goals, priorities, positive attitude and your life's purpose. Continue to think of what you wish to accomplish and how you desire getting there. Think about which tasks are important to complete in the near term and which ones require a bit more time to finish. I invite you to consider all that affects your level of positivity on a daily basis.

These are not empty, meaningless requests when I ask you to apply a bit of mental power in consideration of these important areas in your life. Now that you are thinking about what you do, I ask that you *play to win* as you navigate through life and execute your plan for success.

With every goal that you establish, I encourage you to think like a champion in terms of how you will meet and exceed expectations. With every priority, strategize **how** you will deliver with impact. As a leader, place thoughtful focus upon how your winning attitude and disposition will affect people and situations where you find yourself. You possess great power to make a positive difference.

Playing to win is much more than a cliché. It is both a declarative and a call to action for the way that you operate. Playing to win makes a bold statement about your approach to life. Most champions begin their journey focused upon what they do, how to execute, and engaging with a mindset geared towards winning. You are that same person and can be a champion in your own regard. Develop and maintain your winning attitude my friend and the rest of us will look to see you soar. Though your goals and challenges may be great, in order to reach the top, it is imperative that you play to win.

19

Ignite Greatness with Your Positivity

I will get right to the point. My goal is to motivate and encourage you to bring greater levels of positivity into your life. This advantage can be used to ignite personal greatness that I believe is already within you. Your reaction to my statement could be "…what greatness are you talking about and how does being more positive in my approach to life unleash what is within me?" I am so glad that you asked.

For those already on board and for those who asked the question, I am happy that I am able to engage with you to share a few thoughts regarding positivity. Many of us are limited in what we are able to do and achieve based upon our limited positive thinking, or a total lack thereof. We already know that our thoughts are very powerful and have the ability to set us on a path towards achieving the things that we set out and intend to do. At the same time, our thoughts have the ability to take us captive and render each of us ineffective with whatever we touch. The level of positivity that we bring to the table of life has major implications upon what we think and how we think.

If your thoughts typically have you in a good place then make note of where you currently are. For some, achieving *good* is a struggle and we do not want to overlook that important milestone. Please do not get too comfortable yet. If you remember from my title and my goal, my desire is for you to ignite the greatness that is within you by leveraging your positivity. Now it is time to move beyond good.

Are you one who looks for positive elements within people and in situations where you are engaged? How does your positivity show itself? Are you one to encourage others? Do you use your mental power to think of all the ways that you will accomplish worthwhile goals as opposed to joining the naysayer chorus with all of the reasons why your motivation is a bad idea. Does your level of positivity typically align you with other can-do individuals who refuse to quit in the face of adversity? I could ask many more defining questions; however, I trust that you understand what I am trying to reveal by now. **We can achieve more.**

We have the power to make an incredible difference in our lives and in the lives of others through our positivity and our ability to influence levels of positivity in the environment beginning with each of us. We are wonderfully and uniquely made, each offering a unique perspective which may impact another individual or the world. I encourage you to consider ways that you can bring greater levels of positivity to every situation where you are engaged. In doing so, it is my belief that we are then able to be our best selves. We are able to achieve more and we are then able to help others go further in life. In short, unleashing new levels of positivity can indeed be the key to igniting greatness within you.

There are no "silver bullets" in life and you certainly have options with what I am asking you to consider here.

❖ Option A: Set yourself on a path to intentionally focus upon and choose negativity.

❖ Option B: Choose to do nothing and see how it plays out for you going forward.

❖ Option C: Make the commitment to intentionally infuse greater levels of positivity in all that you do as a path to ignite greatness within you.

I would love to know which option you choose and how that choice worked out for you! Make the right choice to support your continued growth and success.

20

Positive Attitude and F.D.I.C.

I have spent many years working in the financial services industry at large commercial banks. In the financial world, the Federal Deposit Insurance Corporation is in place to instill and promote the public's confidence with depository institutions in the United States. Depositors have protection which insures each account against losses up to a pre-set limit. In a financial sense, FDIC protection is a must have and extremely valuable. I will address a different type of F.D.I.C. and provide insight regarding how to use your positive attitude is an effective tool when dealing with the theme of F.D.I.C.

Life presents each of with a full load to deal with and sometimes it all appears to come to a head in one mighty wave. If this never happens to you then congratulations, you are in the minority. Developing a world-class positive attitude and staying ahead of the negativity curve can be extremely exhausting. If you are not careful, you will find yourself navigating F.D.I.C. in the form of **F**ears, **D**oubts, **I**nsecurity and **C**omplaints.

Situations can cause us to believe in *false* evidence *appearing* *real* or **f**ear. When we buy into fear, feelings of **d**oubt can come into existence. We may begin to question ourselves, our worth and our ability to add value to all that takes place around us. This is a perfect environment for **i**nsecurity to settle into our spirit. Before long, we have a long list of **c**omplaints about our situation and all that stands in the path between where we are and where we desire to be. This is not the valuable type of FDIC one would desire in his or her life.

A positive attitude is your perfect weapon to handle the negative F.D.I.C. A positive mindset is your barrier to keep unwarranted fear out of your mind and doubt on the sideline. With positivity as your ally, you walk with confidence and face challenges with a can-do perspective. Insecurity and complaints have no home in the heart or in the mind of an individual protected by a positive attitude. Your outlook, colored with positivity, allows you to navigate through life with an expectation of greatness from yourself. You are able to view the potential in situations as opposed to only seeing the potential problems presented.

The next time you hear the letters FDIC, I hope that it serves as a reminder of the incredible defense mechanism that you possess to deal with negativity. You should not go down a path laced with fear, doubt, insecurity or complaints. Rise above all negativity that comes your way and soar with your positive attitude as the wind supporting your wings.

Make it a part of your routine to enjoy the earth's beauty with your personal positivity tribe.

Image by Ihor Malytskyi

21

Take the Leap!

I am always intrigued when I hear stories of individuals with truly amazing ideas who seldom or never take any action to begin their quest towards greatness. Leaders possess many attributes which enable his or her success. Among the list, you will always find the descriptor of being *action-oriented*. Greatness which originates in one's mind yet remains there only makes one great in his mind. Success and achievement which remains in one's mind only make her successful in their mental space. My goal is to inspire you to take the leap to go to your next level.

> Noted author Henry David Thoreau made this point in stating, *"We must walk consciously only part way toward our goal and then leap into the dark to our success."*

I drew several meanings from this well-stated verse which aligns with our role as positive leaders.

First, leaders have goals. Leaders know what they are working towards and effective leaders have documented plans to carry them towards their goals. **If your goals are always in vision state without action, you will not achieve them.** My second observation is that walking towards your goals is not nearly enough. Walking conveys that motion is occurring and that one is moving forward, ideally towards goal completion. Merely walking is far deficient in our efforts. You must do more.

My last observation is when taking the leap into darkness, something must happen that is a radical departure from the status quo. If walking is your thing, enjoy the walk. For the type of leader success that I trust you are looking to achieve, it is time to take a leap forward. My last observation comes from the word darkness. At no point does Mr. Thoreau imply that the leap is into anything with certainty. His commentary implies quite the opposite. We must leap into darkness and uncertainty. We must take steps into the unknown, which requires both courage and determination. According to Thoreau, that is where we attain success.

Next levels of success often remain hidden right in front of us. Never far away, just hidden in the dark. You may not realize it yet, however, you were called to project your leadership light into that dark place. Your leadership light will lead you to your success **and** light the path for others. Taking the leap occurs when you feel empowered to move forward and are ready to act. Get ready, get set, take your best leap. I guarantee that your forward leap will position you closer to goal achievement. Success is yours, only when you are willing to take the leap.

22

Negotiating and Contracting from a Position of Positivity

As a part of the human dynamic, we encounter situations whereby we must contract or agree how to move forward to achieve desired goals and results. Sometimes, we are required to negotiate with others. Competing priorities and in some instances a total difference of opinion requires the skillful art of negotiation. We see this in all relationships ranging from a high-level corporate meeting to a parent contracting and negotiating with a child to finish his vegetables at dinner. Few of us are free from the need to engage in contracting or negotiating.

Negotiating from a perspective of power is a well-documented strategy and there are volumes of information detailing how to develop this skill-set. I encourage you to incorporate a strategy of positivity into your arsenal of contracting and negotiation skills. Finding middle ground may not be easy to do. In some situations, there may not be any level of compromise to achieve through negotiation. A reality exists that there may not always be a point of agreement. An important part of my message is that the road to discover a point of compromise and agreement should be approached with a positive mindset.

You may ask, what does this look like? You may approach the task of negotiating by clearly sharing benefits to others while articulating your perspectives. We love to use the moniker of a "win-win" scenario when applicable. Sometimes, there is no "win-win" and one must stand strong upon his or her convictions and beliefs. Even in those scenarios, it is possible to stand strong from a position of power in a positive manner by clearly addressing issues and concerns without engaging in a personal attack.

Not every cloud has a silver lining. Not every situation holds a level of compromise whereby opposing sides are pleased with the outcome. Life is not that simple. **Keep your head above the clouds of negativity and show your strength in a positive manner.** Demonstrate your willingness and capacity to contract and negotiate with others in a way that may move the dialogue forward as opposed to bringing it to a grinding halt. An important consideration to remember is that one side does not have to loose everything in order for the other side to win. Sometimes, we must agree to disagree and go our separate ways. Even under those circumstances, part ways in the most positive way possible and always with respect intact. You may very soon be back at the negotiating table with the very same individuals before you know it and your level of positivity may serve you well.

23

Give the Gift of Positivity

For many, the holiday season is the giving season. You have to look no further than the newspaper, jam-packed with sales papers and bulletins featuring eye-grabbing offers. Online ads pop and populate your screen in effort to entice you to point and click your way to support your need or desire to give. For those who watch any amount of television, between scenes from your favorite show there is a barrage of commercials and infomercials all competing for your attention and your funds.

There is an item that you can still give to those close to you, to complete strangers whom you interact with or to anyone in the world through your contact points. You can give your best self through the level of positivity that you exude. How you react to situations, the way that you choose to engage with others and the way that you respond begins with your attitude and your positivity level. **The choice is yours.** If you choose to lift others up and relate to them in a positive way, what a great gift that you are able to provide. If you choose to leave individuals in a better place after engaging with you than before, you are giving the gift of positivity as only you can deliver.

Yes, most of us immediately enjoy and appreciate tangible gifts that we are able to hold or use as we wish. We have fond memories of cherished toys received as a child or thoughts of special gifts received since childhood. Sometimes, those pleasant memories fade over time as the toy breaks or when we move on from our immediate joy. Give something lasting by sharing your positivity with others. Your sharing can become the gift that keeps on giving throughout the year. Individuals may forget exactly what tangible gift that you gave them, even when given on a special occasion. What has the ability to stay with an individual over time is how you make them feel through your positive and uplifting words of encouragement especially if you deliver them at a time when they need it the most. Put your wallet or purse away and plan a few gifts of positivity then deliver them to others. I encourage you to become a source of positivity that keeps on giving.

24

Unleash Your Super Power

Positive Leader, you may question what in the world I am referring to when I challenge you to unleash your super power. If you were to compare yourself to what one thinks in terms of super power abilities, your thoughts may take you down a path of limits and what you cannot accomplish. You probably cannot fly through the air unassisted. As humans, we lack x-ray vision and the ability to outrun a motorized vehicle at top speed. We cannot reduce a skyscraper to a mountain of rubble with only our bare hands. The list of our mortal limits goes on and on.

Armed with a positive attitude, you are capable of unleashing your personal brand of super power and strength. You are unique and able to look at situations in a way that empowers you to make a unique impact. When interacting with others, your brand of positivity is on display and may bring out the best in them in a super way. **Your personal positivity is your super power!** By leveraging your super power, you can create some amazing outcomes. No need for a flowing cape or a letter on your chest for you to feel that you have super ability. You already have it within your being through the positivity you possess. If you classify yourself as a work in progress, as many of us are, remain committed to increasing your positive power. As your positivity factor increases, so does your ability to make a positive impact.

From this day forward, move with purpose and act with positive confidence. Be the super hero that you are capable of being and unleash positivity as your super power. You will amaze yourself and others in your approach to life and through what you accomplish.

You are a lighthouse and a beacon to inspire and uplift others.

Image by Tony Naccarato

25

The Final Lap

Where did the time go? It seems as though this year was just beginning only yesterday and we are now staring at the closing laps on the horizon. Before we charge off and begin making our future *to-do* list, we owe it to ourselves to finish strong.

In the runner's world, there is a phenomenon known as runner's kick. This simply refers to the strong sprint and burst of energy at the end of the race. We can employ that same mentality in pursuit of the goals that we were so passionate about at the start. In approaching your final lap, are you ready to call upon your final burst of energy to successfully complete your chosen goals?

Take a moment to remind yourself of your priorities and employ your final "kick" to ensure that you complete what you set out to do and that you **finish your race**. Remember, you have trained for this time and you have come too far to throw in the towel now. Kick your way to success, then later we will prepare for our next race.

26

No Excuses

Seldom are great accomplishments completed by individuals who consistently offer excuses. Every excuse counts as a step on the journey away from achieving your goals.

"Ninety-nine percent of failures come from people who have the habit of making excuses."

-George Washington Carver

This day and every day, we must leverage the power of fulfilling our commitment to success and happiness. **Avoid rationalizing and explaining all of the reasons why you can't and focus upon how you can.** Excellence instead of excuses wins every time.

27

Be a Lighthouse
During the Storm

It was a cold, stormy evening on the coast. The sun disappeared many hours ago as the color of the sky migrated from a warm orange glow to a chilling steel-gray appearance. As the waves continued to increase in strength, the captain of the small vessel searched the horizon for a reassuring sight. After hours of searching, the captain was close to giving up. Finally, through the torrential rain, wind, fog and darkness the captain saw what he longed to see. A rescuing beam flashed from a lighthouse on the distant coast was just enough to alter the course and move towards safety. With confidence, he angled the ship and moved into a safe place. Once back in the harbor, all was well and everyone on the ship was safe. This was not the first major storm experienced by the crew, however there was great concern in the midst of the storm.

The lighthouse operator saw the clouds and the storm moving in. Without being prompted or asked, our operator instinctively turned on the beacon to guide ships along the way during the storm. This quick action was the saving grace and enabled the captain to reach safety.

As positive leaders, we are often in situations whereby we are safe however we see those around us in the midst of a storm. It could be a friend, a neighbor, a coworker, a family member or a member of the organization where we serve. We did not cause the storm and we may even experience some of the same effects of what we see others struggling through. Just as it rained off the coast, it also rained on the shoreline. **Lesson one**, life's storms do not always happen in isolation. A similar experience should yield greater empathy into another's stormy situation. Since our captain had been in previous storms, he knew what to look for, yet did not see the beacon for quite a while. Our **second lesson** is that previous storms and victories over them does not guarantee that future storms will not come our way.

Our lighthouse operator followed instinct and protocol by not waiting for a phone call or a request to become involved and help. Once current conditions were acknowledged, engagement began. **Lesson number three** is for us to become engaged in certain situations when our involvement may make a difference in the wellbeing of someone close to us. When you take a chance, you may save a life.

I am urging you to be a lighthouse during someone else's storm. In some instances, you may have no idea that a storm is happening. When you realize that a storm is in progress, take action and help bring those caught between the churning waves back to shore. Shining your light does not mean that you have all the answers. It does not mean that you are always able to offer a complete solution. It does mean that you are not willing to sit motionless when you know that a rescue effort is required. The captain still had to navigate to shore, however he successfully did so with great assistance exactly when help was needed. Your friend will need to do his or her part, however, do your part by giving clues to safety during their life-storm. Take action and move to help just when you see that conditions are rough and require your assistance. Our **last lesson** is that none of us are immune from going through storms and when the next one arrives; you may be the one requiring a lighthouse effort to return to shore. Be the lighthouse in another's storm. As a positive leader, it is the right thing to do.

28

Getting Back on Track

We have seen it happen over and over again. The top salesperson suddenly has a cold-streak. The all-star athlete has a few games whereby he or she struggles to do what was done effortlessly so many times. The leader who previously excelled when articulating clear, concise messages delivered a big *"miss"* during the last team meeting which left many annoyed and confused. In each example, the individual who consistently delivered somehow experienced a rough spot. Each experienced a time when they were off track. Life brings challenges your way, some seen and anticipated. Additionally, we encounter many unforeseen obstacles. Adequate preparation enables us to navigate through and around much of what comes our way. We are not perfect and any of us can get off track in our journey.

When we are out of our lane and off track, we sometimes lose confidence for a short while. We search for solutions and the path to return to our proper place and to the level of performance we are accustomed to demonstrating. As positive leaders, it is important that we prepare to successfully navigate through challenges and difficulties. It is not a matter of if we ever get off track, it becomes a matter of getting back when disruption happens.

I will offer three steps which should help you return to your rightful place when you experience a temporary downturn. *First,* understand that the measure of your success or failure is seldom defined in any a single moment. No one wants to have a string of unsuccessful moments and we wish to always do our best. When challenges are encountered and you are not at your best, try not to place too much pressure upon yourself in the moment. Take time to reflect and correct. My *second* point is for individuals to think about what enabled previous success. In most instances, there is a track record of what worked in the past. **As a part of your reflection, be sure to focus upon what fueled success more than what contributed to a temporary letdown.** This requires you to turn off the negative video of the crash playing over and over in your mind. Learn from the moment, however do not dwell upon what happened. My *third* point has part a and part b, (my way of sneaking in an extra point). Part a involves maintaining a healthy level of personal confidence in yourself. You delivered in the past which serves as your proof point that you are more than capable. Do not doubt your ability or lose confidence. Part b is to positively visualize what will take place when it is your turn once again.

It all begins in your mind. Highly successful individuals see themselves as successful in the moment before the moment arrives and prepare accordingly. Positive images featuring you should run through your mind as opposed to a continuous video of failures.

Are we invincible? Of course not, we all have vulnerabilities. Are we perfect? Undoubtedly not, and perfection is usually an unrealistic goal. **Know that you *can* and *believe* in yourself to make it happen.** Begin with the right thoughts in your mind and maintain the right attitude to deliver at your highest level possible. Maintain faith in your ability and be sure to adequately prepare for your upcoming moment. A positive leader is often judged more critically by what he or she does when the "hiccup" occurs. When we fall down, we need to get back up and get back on track. Let us learn the lesson in the temporary fall and get back to our feet. Leaders get knocked down, then they rise to continue moving forward in a positive manner. Get ready to stand again and deliver again as only you can.

As long as the water remains on the outside, this vessel will survive the stormy seas. Keeping negativity from getting inside of your spirit will enable you to endure life's rough waves. Though adverse conditions may surround you, they do not have to get inside of you.

Image by Jean-Pierre Brungs

29

What are You Working Toward?

We know that goals are important and they should inform the choices we make and the paths we decide to pursue. Our efforts may sometimes appear to be in vain, however, when we set out to achieve anything worthwhile, we increase the likelihood of getting there with documented goals and a plan in place. Stated another way, what we commit to accomplishing defines what we are working toward. Take a moment to consider the things you are striving to achieve. What are your priorities and imperatives? What type of improvements or changes are you looking to claim? Legendary sports superstar and Hall of Famer Julius "Dr. J" Erving, captured this concept in the following statement; *"**Goals determine what you are going to be.**"*

In answering the question what are you working toward, one must understand that goals are what will get you there. Aim high, dream big and set goals that will help transform yourself into the person you strive to become. Remember to gain a great deal of learning along the way. **Success is often born out of falling short and many successful individuals attribute their achievements to the lessons learned through their failed attempts.** Document your goals and go all out to achieve them. Work toward completing your priorities and allow your goals to inform your directions. Your success depends upon it.

30

Positive Planting Yields a Positive Harvest

There were two farmers who lived across the road from each other. One spring, our first farmer followed his annual routine of tilling the ground, treating the soil then planting a wide variety of vegetables that he and his family enjoyed. Once the seeds sprouted, he monitored his garden daily and ensured that sufficient water was delivered for optimal growth. His neighbor, our second farmer, tilled and treated his soil as he readied himself for a productive season. Our second farmer however chose not to plant a wide variety of vegetables. In fact, he only planted one type of seeds and did so sparsely. He often forgot to check on the progress of his garden and did very little to have a productive season.

By now, I am thinking you already know the outcome of both of our farmers. Our first farmer planted with a purpose, nurtured his seedlings, removed weeds and had a very productive harvest. He was extremely proud of his accomplishments and his family enjoyed eating the tasty vegetables. Our second farmer put minimal effort and care into his garden and achieved minimal production. The plants that did bear edible products only had small yields. The products never reached full potential. They were choked out by the destructive weeds and received minimal water. At harvest time, we had two very different outcomes as a result of each individual's actions at the beginning and throughout the growing season.

Using this short story, gardening is an ideal analogy to make a few observations about how positivity can work in your favor. Planting seeds of positivity into your life and into the lives of others has the potential to yield a positive harvest. Our second farmer put forth very little effort to prepare for his success. Perhaps tilling the ground compares to examining relationships with others or turning over soiled relationships symbolic with kicking off a new season of life. The annual routine began, however farmer number two did not sow seeds in a wise manner. We experience the same result when we begin the process of examining our touchpoints and relationships, then minimize positive outcomes when we fail to sow seeds of positivity.

With a decision such as this, why should our second farmer have expected to have a plentiful harvest? When we fail to plant positive seeds, we should not expect positive outcomes. What are the seeds of positivity that I am referring to? Seeds may be as simple as delivering a kind word to someone else at the right time. It may be a smile or encouragement when someone needs it the most. Positive seeds may be found in doing a good deed for another person or as simple as taking the time to listen to someone in the midst of a challenge. We should be intentional in our efforts to uplift and inspire others. If a few random outcomes, or plants, do appear it is the result of random success which is not sustainable. There is something to be said about nurturing what is planted, which aids the harvest. Whether discussing a garden or relationships, we must ensure that the right amount of light is available. We must observe and water when necessary to replenish and refresh relationships with others. **Occasionally, we must take the time to weed-out undesirable people and situations from our lives or risk having our growth impaired or being denied the nutrients and benefits which were intended for us.**

When we sow positively and plentifully, we should live with an expectation of an abundantly positive harvest. Once we plant seeds of positivity, we must nurture and care for our seedlings to allow the roots to dive deep into the soil for continued nourishment, growth and stability. We cannot afford to plant seeds of positivity then walk away thinking that all will work out perfectly. Farming is hard work. Laboring to create positive outcomes requires time, effort and attention to details.

I ask that you keep this story of our farmers top-of-mind. Consider the type of harvest you desire reaping. Consider the level of commitment necessary to achieve the outcome that you have in mind. While you will directly benefit from the plentiful harvest of positivity, so will those closest to you. Remember, our first farmer enjoyed the tasty items at harvest and so did his family. The same can be stated regarding what happens when benefits of planting positivity seeds are realized during our harvest season. Your family and those within your inner circle will likely feast with you.

Time for a review; be sure to prepare, plant, nourish, care, eliminate weeds on the way to your harvest. Roll up your sleeves and get ready to put forth the effort to ensure that you and those around you will take part in the feast as a result of your efforts. My final point to encourage you to follow this path is my reminder that winter is coming. The literal winter season is when nothing grows, cold weather abounds and one must hope for the prospect of a bountiful crop. In the figurative sense, winter may be a season of personal hardship, extreme challenges or a time when each of us desires to feel the warmth of a summer day in our lives. In either example, we need to prepare to "eat" during the winter. Sowing seeds of positivity in abundance can influence a great harvest with enough positivity to get you through the winter on your horizon. Which side of the road do you prefer to live?

31

Ships, Subs and Positivity

Take a few minutes to think about ships on the mighty seas and submarines that cruise the depths of the oceans. Both are engineered to sail and cruise through all types of weather and through turbulent currents. While facing grueling winds, chilling temperatures and relentless waves all around, ships and subs successfully complete their journey. The sheer size of the oceans and seas make even the largest vessels appear miniscule by comparison. One could easily think that these amazing engineered wonders would not have a chance to remain afloat or successfully dive without facing major challenges.

Though surrounded by water, a ship or a sub remains safe as long as the water remains outside of the vessel. Whether being wildly tossed in a storm or when submerged beneath the surface, all is well as long as the water is kept from entering. We must employ the same preventive position to keep negativity from entering our minds and taking over our thoughts. Life can sometimes cause us to feel as though we are floating in an ocean of negativity with wave after wave crashing against us. When situations take a turn for the worse, we may feel as though we are in *"submarine mode"*, navigating below the surface. In times such as these, it becomes imperative that you use your world-class positive attitude to keep negativity on the outside.

Remaining positive does not mean that you are in denial of all of the negative people or negative influences surrounding you.

Negativity truly exists in many people and less than positive situations can happen quite often. In the same manner as ships and subs operate, you are able to survive the rough seas and ocean depths of negativity. While hard work, planning and continuous effort are required, you can indeed keep from sinking due to an overabundance of negativity from entering your life. Beware of the smallest leaks or cracks in your *mental hull* that will allow even small amounts of negative water to enter. It only takes one point of entry for negative water to eventually overtake you and place you in a dangerous position. Surely, you may continue making forward progress, however it becomes a matter of time before progress is impaired and you are deep into survival mode.

You were built to endure the rough seas of life and win! With all that is happening around you, remain encouraged and leverage all of the positivity that you possess. There will be many picturesque days when the warm sunshine guides your journey. Even when the sun shines on the deck of a ship, water still surrounds it on all sides. Your mission is to keep the negative water on the outside. Feeling underwater should not cause us to give up. We have to keep our mental hull intact and apply enough positive pressure to keep negativity out and prevent ourselves from being crushed by negative pressure.

I wish you many days of smooth sailing and cruising ahead. When the waters become rough or when you feel as though you are submerged by the depths of negativity, remain afloat and keep what is outside of you from overtaking you. Employ strength, resilience and determination as a positive leader should do. Last but not least, icebergs do exist. Remember, an iceberg only shows a small portion of what may harm you. Look for the warning signs and understand that a negative situation, an iceberg, provides a much greater threat than you may initially perceive. Chart your course through life carefully and do your part to successfully navigate your ocean. Do not allow the volume of negativity to overwhelm you. All remains well as long as you keep negativity from sinking you. Bon Voyage!

32

Necessary Change

Many of us at some point in our lives have either chased butterflies as they came close to us as a child or admired their graceful beauty and seemingly effortless flight. Butterflies are amazing creatures and their beauty is one of many reasons to appreciate them. As we know, the life of a butterfly is not always one of splendor and beauty. Before soaring through the air currents, each butterfly must endure a ground existence. Day after day, they navigate through tall grass, brush, climb trees, all while ignoring the sky. You see, there is something inside the caterpillar that keeps them marching, eating and preparing for future greatness. The butterfly knows that the ground existence is only temporary and that their moment in the sun is on the way.

In order to progress from ground level to soaring in the summer breeze, an amazing metamorphosis must occur. When the time is right, the caterpillar realizes that the time for crawling around is over. The tiny creature has enjoyed its fill of grass and leaves as a bottom-feeder and finds an ideal place to begin the change. The caterpillar creates a cocoon and seals itself in from the rest of the world. It is only when inside and fully constrained can change occur. When it is time to emerge, a new creature comes out and experiences the world for the first time. It is necessary for the transformation to take place in order for the world to marvel at the beauty of the butterfly.

As positive leaders, there are a few lessons that we observe from the butterfly that may help us through some of the stages and seasons in our own lives. *First*, we should always keep in mind that any current ground situation is never permanent. Just like the caterpillar, we sometimes have to do a lot of "ground-level" crawling around just to survive. See this time as more than mere survival, it is a time when we should prepare for something greater. Our *second* lesson is that we instinctively will know when we must undergo necessary change. Life as you view it prior to your transformation suddenly is no longer capable of sustaining you and all that is within you waiting for the right moment to burst and come forth. Lesson number *three* teaches us that in many instances, we may feel the most constrained just prior to our moment of glory. That is the time when you really discover what you are made of. Doubts and fears may set in when you hear others around you having a ball, yet you remain constrained and bound to wait your turn. How many times have we felt as though we were about to burst while waiting for our big moment to dance in the sunlight? **Sometimes, in order to make that next transformational step, one must shut out all of the noise from the world and experience a period of quiet growth.**

Our next lesson teaches us that necessary change allows us to come through the challenging transformation and emerge as a work of wonder and beauty. Initially, the butterfly must still crawl. Even nature has a way of reminding its creatures where they came from before taking flight. We too must hone our skills and allow our wings to dry before taking flight and showing the world all that we are capable of. **When our time is right and after we have been transformed, we soar**. We glide on the breeze and experience an entirely new existence, just as the butterfly does. Viewing this fantastic being would be impossible without enduring necessary change.

How does your life compare to the stages that our caterpillar went through on the way to flying and soaring? Are you in a temporary phase of ground existence or are you feeling a bit overly constrained for the moment? Maintain your confidence and your level of positivity while knowing that you are going through necessary change. When you come out, after having experienced transformation, get ready to dazzle the world with your beauty, grace, newly minted skills and all that you have to offer.

I urge you to be at peace in your current stage and know that your change is on the way. At a point in your journey, you may feel tied-down and constrained, however remain resilient. Your day of glory is on the way. Come forth and leave your mark upon the world as every positive leader should do. Here is the final lesson. The butterfly never even has to make a sound to demonstrate all of the beauty and purpose that was unleashed through necessary change. The caterpillar simply went to work and committed each day towards preparing for the future. The butterfly ignored all of the messages that communicated lack and the inability to fly. Can you say that you have that same level of resolve? Surely you do! **Let your positivity compel you to reach higher, destroy challenges and keep you on the path which leads to your positive transformation.** The world is waiting to see you explore new boundaries with new capabilities.

33

Keep Your Fire Burning

We have seen the scenario play out over and over when an individual begins a project or an initiative highly energized, highly motivated and on a path to lead with impact. There is "pep" in their step and they move and operate with purpose. Seemingly, nothing will interfere nor deter them from delivering with impact. Then, life happens and fatigue begins to settle in. On occasion, doubt and disbelief may enter the mind. My intention is not to create an all-inclusive list of everything that could disrupt success. I used a few examples to demonstrate that each of us encounter real issues that can threaten our ability to reach and exceed our goals. We may find ourselves in a place where the raging fire that we began with has been reduced to a smoldering mess at best.

As life and competing priorities come at us fast, our challenge is to keep our fire burning. **We have to ensure that we start strong, endure the journey then finish strong.** Distractions are real and it is never a question of what happens if distractions enter the picture. The focus should always be upon how you will navigate myriad distractions that come your way. In the most fatal scenario, a distraction may totally derail your efforts.

Several actions will help you keep your fire burning and assist you in keeping your fire stoked. Written goals and visual reminders are an excellent way to keep what is important in front of you.

Statistics show that individuals with written goals that are regularly reviewed are more likely to achieve them compared to individuals who only think about them occasionally. Post notes in place where you can see your goals often as reminders and by all means, use your technology to send you reminders regularly. A second technique is to share your goals and passions with an accountability partner. Success should be shared, so elicit help from another trusted person who will help and encourage you when the flames appear to diminish.

My last suggestion is to remain grounded throughout your journey. While we should not charge off and head down our path oblivious to all that is happening around us, we cannot afford to become distracted with every "flavor of the day." In other words, **stay true to your cause, never forget your purpose and tie your actions to what you are trying to achieve.** Sometimes, this may include watching out for the winds of change that come your way. Change may be good and the anticipation of change should always be considered. Even in the face of change, consider the effect upon your fire and how you may need to adjust along the way.

Stay true to your cause, remind yourself regularly of your "why" and anticipate what may be on the horizon. Doing all of this may seem intense and exhausting. Delivering with impact requires intense focus and execution of the activities which support our success. Take what began as a mere spark to the next level and keep your fire burning.

Positivity = Freedom

Image by Glen Carrie

Parting Thoughts

As author of *Positive Leader: Reflections and Motivations*, it was my pleasure writing and sharing my thoughts and perspectives with you. It is my desire to compel you to make a positive difference in your life through my reflections and motivations. My goal is to always write with a purpose and if you are able to gain usable value from my writing, I will claim that as purpose achieved. Positivity carries each of us much further than negative momentum. For those looking for an extra edge towards a positive state of mind, allow Reflections and Motivations to make a difference in your life.

Ideally, this work presents much more than a good read only in terms of entertainment value. I challenge you to move forward and commit yourself to integrating as many of the suggestions and inspirations into your daily routine as possible. Regardless of whether we gain from reflecting or from being motivated, our goal is to learn the lesson then apply it as we move forward. Either reflecting or being motivated can be a powerful influence upon our success and the positive outcomes we have the potential to create.

Our parting is only temporary and I look forward to sharing more Reflections and Motivations with you before too long. Since real dialogue is a two-way affair, feel free to share your thoughts and insights with me via email at **info@infinityleadershipconsulting.org** subject line **Reflections and Motivations-My Journey**. Leverage your social media platform of choice to let the world know all about your discoveries and revelations along the way. Use this tool to carry you forward. I believe in the power of positivity and that a positive mindset will elevate you to the next level in your life.

Positive Leader...make it happen!

Image Acknowledgements

All photographic images are owned and credited by the following individuals in accordance with the licensing agreement and may be located at https://unsplash.com

Clark Tibbs	page xiv
Janusz Maniak	page 8
Martin Fennema	page 18
Sharon Pittaway	page 28
Benedicto de Jesus	page 36
Ihor Malytskyi	page 46
Tony Naccarato	page 55
Jean-Pierre Brungs	page 62
Glen Carrie	page 74

CPSIA information can be obtained
at www.ICGtesting.com
Printed in the USA
LVHW050849120121
676265LV00005B/290

9 781977 205612